KILLERS OF THE ANIMAL KINGDOM

LIONS

JILL KEPPELER

PowerKiDS
press

New York

Published in 2020 by The Rosen Publishing Group, Inc.
29 East 21st Street, New York, NY 10010

First Edition

Editor: Elizabeth Krajnik
Book Design: Reann Nye

Photo Credits: Cover, p. 22 Eric Isselee/Shutterstock.com; p. 4 Olga_i/Shutterstock.com; p. 5 Kakuli/Shutterstock.com; p. 6 Glass and Nature/Shutterstock.com; p. 7 COULANGES/Shutterstock.com; p. 8 apple2499/Shutterstock.com; p. 9 Maggy Meyer/Shutterstock.com; p. 11 Chris Minihane/Moment/Getty Images; p. 12 Image captured by Joanne Hedger/Moment/Getty Images; p. 13 Jason Prince/Shutterstock.com; p. 15 Catalin Mitrache/500px/Getty Images; p. 16 Ivan Mateev/Shutterstock.com; p. 17 Mogens Trolle/Shutterstock.com; p. 18 Eugene Troskie/Shutterstock.com; p. 19 Wolfgang Kaehler/LightRocket/Getty Images; p. 20 LeonP/Shutterstock.com; p. 21 MONIRUL BHUIYAN/AFP/Getty Images.

Library of Congress Cataloging-in-Publication Data

Names: Keppeler, Jill, author.
Title: Lions / Jill Keppeler.
Description: New York : PowerKids Press, [2020] | Series: Killers of the
  animal kingdom | Includes index.
Identifiers: LCCN 2019006151| ISBN 9781725306134 (paperback) | ISBN
  9781725306158 (library bound) | ISBN 9781725306141 (6 pack)
Subjects: LCSH: Lion–Juvenile literature.
Classification: LCC QL737.C23 K47 2020 | DDC 599.757–dc23
LC record available at https://lccn.loc.gov/2019006151

Manufactured in the United States of America

CPSIA Compliance Information: Batch #CSPK19. For Further Information contact Rosen Publishing, New York, New York at 1-800-237-9932.

CONTENTS

POWERFUL CATS

Have you ever watched a pet cat **stalk** a toy? It will move carefully and quietly, hiding behind furniture or other cover, getting closer and closer, and then... **pounce**! Lions are much bigger **relatives** of pet cats, but they hunt their **prey** in much the same way.

Lions are powerful big cats, with strong **muscles**, sharp claws, and deadly teeth. They need to eat a lot of meat to keep going! A female lion needs about 11 pounds (5 kg) of meat a day, while a male lion needs about 15.4 pounds (7 kg). That means they need to be good killers.

Lions usually hunt and eat big animals that weigh 100 to 1,000 pounds (45.4 to 453.6 kg), such as zebra and antelope.

5

PRIDE LANDS

Many years ago, lions had a much larger **range** than they do now. They lived across Europe, Africa, and Asia. Today, however, they mostly live in parts of Africa, south of the Sahara Desert. A small group of lions lives in India.

KILLER FACTS

Asiatic lions are the only lions that live in the forest. They live in India's Gir Forest National Park. There are only about 500 of them left.

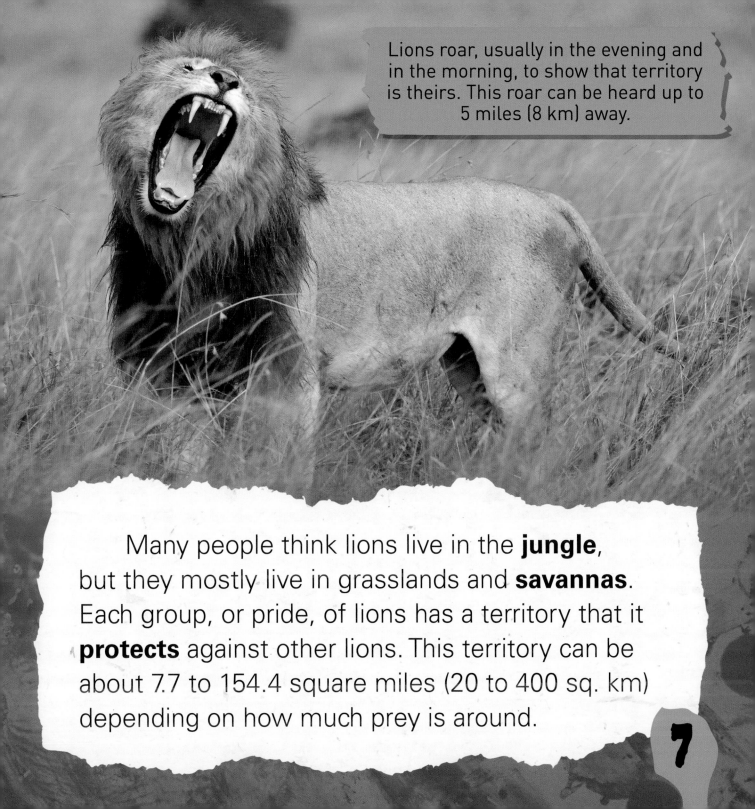

Lions roar, usually in the evening and in the morning, to show that territory is theirs. This roar can be heard up to 5 miles (8 km) away.

Many people think lions live in the **jungle**, but they mostly live in grasslands and **savannas**. Each group, or pride, of lions has a territory that it **protects** against other lions. This territory can be about 7.7 to 154.4 square miles (20 to 400 sq. km) depending on how much prey is around.

7

KING OF THE BEASTS

You may have heard the lion called "the king of beasts." Male lions are bigger than female lions. They can be about 6 to 10 feet (1.8 to 3 m) long, not counting their tail. They can stand about 4 feet (1.2 m) tall and can weigh up to 500 pounds (226.8 kg).

KILLER FACTS

Despite their nickname, lions are often smaller than tigers. Siberian (Amur) tigers are the biggest tigers. They can weigh up to 660 pounds (299.4 kg) and be up to 13 feet (4 m) long!

SIBERIAN TIGER

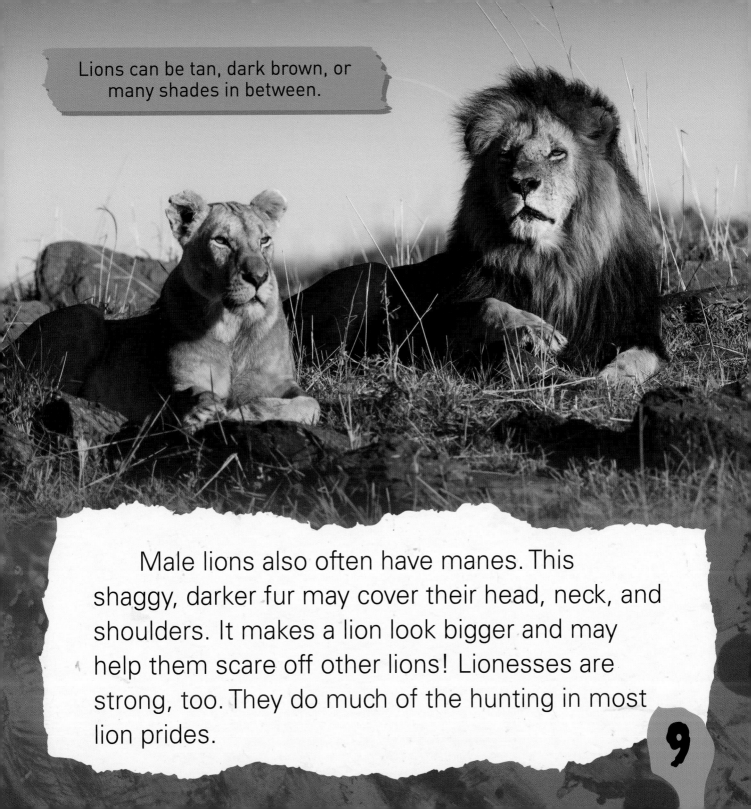

Lions can be tan, dark brown, or many shades in between.

Male lions also often have manes. This shaggy, darker fur may cover their head, neck, and shoulders. It makes a lion look bigger and may help them scare off other lions! Lionesses are strong, too. They do much of the hunting in most lion prides.

9

QUEENS OF THE SAVANNA

Each pride of lions can have up to 40 members, but the average pride has 15 lions. There will be one or a few adult males, plus many lionesses and their cubs. All the lionesses in a pride are related. There are **generations** of lionesses in a single pride!

Lionesses usually are the main hunters in a lion pride. They also raise their cubs together. Sometimes the male lions help with hunts, but their main duty is to guard the pride and its land. Lionesses may hold the same land for years, passing it down to younger generations.

KILLER FACTS

Lions are social creatures. They're the only cats that live in groups. Members of a pride usually form smaller groups within a pride.

10

The lionesses in a pride may include grandmothers, mothers, daughters, and sisters.

11

CUBS TO KILLERS

In the wild, lionesses have **litters** of one to six cubs about every two years. Lionesses in the same pride often have cubs around the same time and raise them together. Lion cubs are tiny and blind when they're born, but they grow fast! They're able to eat meat when they're about three months old. Cubs start taking part in hunts when they're about a year old.

Lion cubs have dark spots when they're born. These spots disappear as the cub gets older.

Most lionesses will stay with the pride when they're grown. Male lions usually leave the pride when they're about three years old. They live alone or with other males unless they take over a pride when they get older.

MIGHTY HUNTERS?

Lionesses hunt and kill big animals. They have to if they're going to feed the pride! But the truth is, lions aren't very **efficient** hunters. Many of their hunts fail. Like your pet cat, lions stalk their prey from a place that hides them and then run at their prey. They run very fast, up to 50 miles (81 km) per hour, but this pace tires them quickly. Most prey gets away.

When a lion or lioness does catch prey, it jumps on the animal and bites its neck until the animal goes down. A pride usually hunts at night, from around sunset to sunrise.

KILLER FACTS

Lions sometimes steal kills from other animals, including wild dogs and cheetahs. They'll also eat carrion, which is meat from animals that were already dead.

Lionesses hunt in groups. Members may circle a group of animals and then attack from different directions.

WHAT'S FOR DINNER?

Lions often hunt wildebeests, zebras, and antelopes. When they can't find bigger prey, they'll hunt smaller animals, even **rodents**, but since lions need so much meat, they mostly hunt larger creatures. Sometimes, a pride will even take down a giraffe or an elephant, but this usually only happens if they find a young or sick one.

Lions can be very messy eaters! They often fight over food.

Right after a kill, the male lions eat first, followed by the lionesses, and then the cubs. An adult lion can eat more than 75 pounds (34 kg) of meat at a single meal! Then it won't need to eat again for a while.

17

PEOPLE VS. LIONS

For the most part, lions don't hunt humans. However, they're predators. If they're hungry and they need food, they might attack humans. There are about 200 to 250 lions attacks on humans a year. The number of attacks could go up as humans continue to move into lions' territories.

18

In 2015, a lion killed a woman in South Africa. The woman had rolled down her window while on a car tour of the area.

Lions are an apex predator. This means that they're at the top of the food chain and don't have any natural predators. However, humans have become a danger to lions. People hunt lions and animals tamed by humans, such as dogs, can spread deadly diseases to lions.

19

Lions need a lot of room to hunt, in part because they eat so much meat. However, they're losing their **habitats** to people. Lions hunt people's farm animals, and people shoot them or poison them because of that. If this continues, lions could go extinct. This means they would completely die out.

The number of lions has decreased by 40 percent over the past three generations. There are now only about 20,000 in the wild. This isn't just bad for the lions. As an apex predator, they keep a balance in the number of prey animals in their habitat.

KILLER FACTS

Lions are considered a vulnerable species, or kind, of animal. This means they face a high risk, or danger, of dying out.

Lions live on only a tiny part of the land they used to live on. Some people are trying to help save lions and their habitats.

LION TALES

Lions have been in stories and artwork for many years. Some of this artwork is very old. There are cave paintings with lions in France's Chauvet Cave. They date from about 30,000 years ago. The ancient Egyptians used lions in much of their art. Sekhmet was a lion-headed Egyptian goddess of war.

However, today, lions are in danger, mostly due to human activity. Some people are trying to save them by asking for laws to protect lion territories and lions themselves. Lions are an amazing and important part of our world. They need to be protected!

GLOSSARY

efficient: Capable of producing desired results without wasting materials, time, or energy.

generation: A group of individuals born about the same time.

habitat: The natural place where an animal lives.

jungle: A tropical forest with many plants and trees.

litter: A group of baby animals born to a mother animal all at one time.

muscle: A part of the body that produces motion.

pounce: To jump suddenly toward or onto something.

prey: An animal hunted by other animals for food.

protect: To keep safe.

range: The area of land or water where a species of animal might live.

relative: A member of a family, such as a mother or cousin.

rodent: A small, furry animal with large front teeth, such as a mouse or rat.

savanna: A grassland with scattered patches of trees.

stalk: To follow something while moving slowly and quietly.

INDEX

WEBSITES

Due to the changing nature of Internet links, PowerKids Press has developed an online
list of websites related to the subject of this book. This site is updated regularly. Please
use this link to access the list: www.powerkidslinks.com/kotak/lions